Making Wildlife Ponds

How to create a pond
to attract wildlife to your garden

Jenny Steel

Making Wildlife Ponds - How to create a pond to attract wildlife to your garden
Gardening with Nature Series
Copyright © Jenny Steel 2016

All Rights Reserved
No part of this book may be reproduced in any form
by photocopying or by any electronic or mechanical means,
including information, storage or retrieval systems,
without permission in writing from both the copyright
owner and the publisher of this book.

Jenny Steel has asserted her right under the Copyright,
Design and Patent Act, 1988, to be identified as author of this work.

A CIP catalogue record for this book is available from the British Library

ISBN 9781908241481

First published in 2016 by
Brambleby Books Ltd. UK
Reprinted in 2018, 2019 and 2020
10 9 8 7 6 5 4
www.bramblebybooks.co.uk

Cover design and layout by Tanya Warren, Creatix Design
Cover photo by Jenny Steel

Printed and bound by Cambrian Printers, UK
FSC and PFSC accredited

Making Wildlife Ponds

Male damselfly

About the Author

Jenny Steel developed a passion for wildlife when she discovered caterpillars at the age of six and an interest in birds and wildflowers soon followed. Her mother's enthusiasm for gardening and her father's part-time occupation in journalism and photography were also instrumental in her career path.

A degree in Applied Biology was followed by a Master's Degree in Plant Ecology based on her research into woodland ecosystems in Wytham Woods, Oxford University's well-studied 'outdoor laboratory'. More work in the University's Department of Plant Sciences followed and concluded with a six-year project studying arable weeds.

In 1990 she left the University to set up a wildflower nursery, providing native plants and insect-attracting cottage garden plants for wildlife gardeners. Her writing career began with regular pieces in the award-winning *Limited Edition Magazine*, a sister publication to *the Oxford Times*, and she became a regular contributor to BBC Radio Oxford. More writing work followed for a variety of publications, including *Organic Gardening Magazine*, *The Countryman*, *Spaces Magazine*, *BBC Gardens Illustrated* and *BBC Easy Gardening*. She appeared on the BBC gardening programmes *Gardener's World* and as a presenter on *How Does Your Garden Grow*.

In 2005, she moved from her native Oxfordshire to South Shropshire where she and her husband have created a 2-acre wildlife garden. She is a keen photographer, and her writing and images are inspired by the wildlife and countryside around her and further afield.

Preface

I grew up in Oxford where my mother tended a tiny garden at the back of a Victorian terrace with great passion and skill. This garden at various times housed chickens and bantams, a pond full of Great Crested Newts, borders of prize-winning Dahlias and bumblebee nests. Swifts and House Sparrows nested under the eaves and Robins in the rose arch. These early years established my interest in wildlife as an integral part of a garden, although at that time the term 'wildlife gardening' hadn't been invented.

In spite of living in the middle of a small city, my parents were both country folk, and as a family our focus was on the local countryside or the stately river that runs through Oxford's centre. It was a short walk from my home to the water meadows alongside the Thames at Iffley, in spring a swathe of Lady's Smock and Ragged Robin. As a family we made a yearly pilgrimage to Otmoor or Ducklington to see the fritillary meadows full of the chequered bells of this beautiful plant together with, in my memory at least, acres of Cowslips. The Bluebell woods of the Chilterns were also a regular haunt. I grew up with all this around me but didn't at the time realise how much these walks and visits would influence my career path.

Once I had a home and garden of my own I began to appreciate how important my early gardening and wildlife experiences had been. As much

A garden pond designed for wildlife

Preface

Broad-bodied Chaser Dragonfly

as I loved the plants I was growing, my real interest was in the wildlife that visited these plants and encouraging birds, mammals and invertebrates into my successively larger and larger gardens became an objective, even though at the time this was seen as rather odd! Each garden had a range of habitats and central to those was a wildlife pond.

Gardening for wildlife is no longer a rather out-of-the-ordinary interest and many gardeners now take account of or cater for the wild creatures that visit their garden. One easy way of encouraging wildlife to visit and use our gardens is to create a wildlife pond – something small and tucked away at the end of the garden, much like my first little pond in a small wildlife garden in suburban Oxford or, if you have the space, a larger natural-looking pond surrounded by wetland plants and wildflower meadows, the focal point of my current garden in Shropshire.

Much of the wildlife that visits a garden will benefit from readily available water, whether it is the local fox searching for a reliable source of clean drinking water, a small flock of urban House Sparrows needing a bath, or frogs and toads searching for a breeding place in early spring. Water in the garden also provides a place to grow some of our most beautiful native wetland plants, such as Purple Loosestrife or Water Mint, both of which are useful nectaring sources for summer butterflies. Lastly, and perhaps equally importantly, a garden wildlife pond provides a place to sit, relax, watch and appreciate the wildlife that depend on these important oases.

Male Chaffinch using a bird bath

Common Frog

Contents

CHAPTER ONE
An Introduction to Wildlife Ponds 13

CHAPTER TWO
Ponds in Gardens 17
    Your pond as part of a larger habitat 18

CHAPTER THREE
Pond Creation 23
    Choosing your site 25
    Sun or shade? 28
    What type of lining? 30
    Timing 31
    Designing the shape 32
    Getting started 33
    Making a meadow or creating a bank 33
    Digging the hole 34
    Measuring up for the liner 35
    Lining the pond 36
    Filling the pond 37
    The habitat edges 39

CHAPTER FOUR
Planting your Pond 41
    Natives or non-natives 42
    Sources of plants 43
    Types of plants 44
    How to plant 48
    Avoid at all costs! 49

CHAPTER FIVE
Pond Wildlife 51
    Amphibians 53
    Reptiles 54
    Larger Insects 54
    Smaller Animals 56
    Mammals 56
    Birds 56
    Fish 58

Contents

Predators 58
Wildlife and the law. 59

CHAPTER SIX
Pond Maintenance 61
 Spring and summer 61
 Autumn 62
 Winter 64
 Repairing leaks 65
 Repairing a built-up of silt 66
 Renovating your pond completely 66
 Maintenance of the area around the pond 67

CHAPTER SEVEN
Pond Alternatives 69
 Starting small 69
 A water feature 70
 A mini-pond 70
 Bog gardens 73
 Adapting an existing pond 76

IN CONCLUSION 77
WILDFLOWERS TO CREATE A NATURAL-LOOKING POND . . 78
FURTHER INFORMATION
 Suppliers of pond plants 79
 Further Reading 79

Native White Water Lily

Emperor Dragonfly

Countryside pond with a shady willow

A wild agricultural pond

CHAPTER ONE
An Introduction to Wildlife Ponds

Ponds have always been significant and important features in the British landscape. Yet over the last 100 years or so, the numbers of ponds in our countryside and villages have declined by as much as a half, and with that decline much of the wildlife associated with these watery habitats has also decreased. Frogs, toads, newts and dragonflies are just a few of the more obvious creatures that have suffered from this habitat loss. Underneath the cool water surface of our wild ponds, a whole host of protozoans, invertebrates, including molluscs, and amphibians and fishes have gone for good as their habitat has disappeared, whilst our native birds and mammals have also suffered from this decline.

Not so long ago every village had its pond and every farm had several. Often constructed of puddled clay, these were important areas for the watering of animals, as well as places that played a crucial part in rural life.

Common Frog

A female Common Darter

Alderfly

Alderfly eggs

13

Introduction

A village pond

A garden wildlife pond

In the recent past, the village pond and the village green were areas for recreation and getting together, where ducks were fed and people sat and talked while enjoying the wildlife round about them.

The word 'pond' originally came from the Anglo-Saxon 'pound', meaning an enclosure, and the village pond was a place where water was held for use by both the local people and their animals.

Its uses were many and varied – from fire fighting, when many roofs were thatched, to providing a source of food (ducks and fish) for the local population plus every village blacksmith needed water nearby. Now, however, more than half of our 'natural' country ponds have been filled in, drained or sometimes polluted. Animals can be provided with fresh drinking water more easily via the mains supply, and many old village ponds have been neglected or have been

A safe bathing place for young Bluetits

Introduction

invaded by reeds and rushes, leaving no open water as a wildlife habitat.

These changes in our countryside mean that ponds in our gardens now have a very special role as far as native wildlife is concerned. They provide a safe and permanent breeding place for amphibians and many invertebrates. They act as a watering hole for mammals and, if constructed correctly, somewhere birds can drink and bathe in safety. They offer a home to wetland wildflowers enabling them to establish and bloom.

Everyone can help our native aquatic wildlife and contribute to the conservation of birds, animals and wildflowers by constructing a pond, however small, in their garden. Furthermore, a pond like this will be the focal point of your whole garden, creating fun and interest for everyone who has the time to sit and watch.

Marsh Marigold or Kingcup - ideal for a garden pond

A place to sit and watch

The focal point of a wildlife garden

15

Garden ponds – a place where frogs come to breed in the spring

CHAPTER TWO
Ponds in Gardens

Having looked at the importance of ponds in our countryside and also glimpsed the alarming rate at which they have disappeared and are continuing to disappear, it is hardly surprising that ponds in gardens have become such vital habitats for our native wetland wildlife. Anyone who already has a garden pond will appreciate the fun, interest and opportunities for education this feature can generate for young and old alike. When I was a child our tiny garden was never without a pond of some sort, always brimming with a huge range of interesting wildlife, from dragonfly nymphs and Common Newts to frog tadpoles, sticklebacks and even a couple of native crayfish for a short while. As a keen angler, my father brought home a couple of these once common crustaceans to show me. They spent a day or two in our concrete lined pond before they were returned to their local wild habitat. I was thrilled to see these interesting creatures close up.

The native wildlife that inhabited or visited this very basic pond stimulated my interest and enthusiasm for natural history. I always had a selection of small creatures from the pond in a tiny aquarium in the house and it was here that I watched a male stickleback courting a female and building an underwater nest, marvelled

Dragonfly larval cases...

...after the dragonflies have emerged and flown away.

Great Diving Beetle

A small natural-looking wildlife pond

at frighteningly ugly dragonfly larvae and learnt that water beetles could fly! The hours spent looking at drops of pond water under an old microscope opened up an even smaller and more fascinating world.

It has been estimated that around one in ten gardens has a pond of some description, but not all will be adapted for use by wildlife. Some creatures will use them however they have been made as long as they can get in and out of the water, but other wildlife, particularly newts and toads, may be absent. If you already have a conventional garden pond you might prefer it to be more wildlife friendly or you may want to modify it to be particularly attractive to one type of creature, for instance dragonflies. Encouraging garden birds to drink and bathe may be of special interest. It is possible to customise almost any pond to make it a favoured habitat for all types of wildlife visitor and there is information in Chapter 7 about adapting an existing garden pond, however small, to encourage more varied wildlife visitors and also tips on how to make it safer for mammals and birds.

Your pond as part of a larger habitat

Gardeners tend to think of a wildlife pond as a very important feature, and of course it will be a focal point for you, your family and your wildlife visitors. But it is worth remembering that to the mammals, invertebrates, birds and amphibians that use it your pond is just a small part of a much larger habitat which includes your whole garden and other gardens about you. When constructing a new wildlife pond, it is vital to consider this special feature in relation to the other areas around it, which are all important for the survival of many of the creatures that are moving in and out of the water from one garden habitat to another. This means that when you design a wildlife pond you should give some thought to the surrounding areas and not necessarily construct it in the most convenient spot. Chapter 3 on Pond Creation will give you some ideas about where the best places are in your garden to create a pond or other type of wetland area, but it is good to consider all the other types of habitat round about before you start. In order to do this, we need to look at the more general requirements of the wildlife that will be using it.

The habitat surrounding your pond is important

Native marginal wildflowers

Hedgehogs rely on garden ponds for water

Blackbird about to have a bath.

Bugle - a wildflower suitable for pond edge or bog garden

A garden pond in isolation will very likely be used by frogs for breeding, but the young froglets, once they have developed their legs and want to move from their watery nursery habitat to dry land, can end up as prey for many different creatures including Hedgehogs, some birds, especially Blackbirds, and even toads. It is nature's way that many of them should be eaten and they serve as an important link in the garden food chain. If they weren't providing food for other creatures our gardens would be knee-deep in frogs in no time at all! However, you do want a proportion of them to survive to maturity to increase the frog population in your area. A garden pond surrounded by very short turf, or even a paved pond edge, popular in the recent past, has few hiding places for a small vulnerable froglet. Indeed, many young frogs can leap out of the water onto hot paving on a warm summer's day, either to be snapped up by a hungry Blackbird or to be cooked on the baking stones. Far better then that, they can creep off into a slightly wilder habitat of long cool grasses, amongst creeping plants such as Bugle in a bog garden, or best of all hide under a pile of shady damp logs nearby.

On the other hand, your pond does need to have open and easy access for hedgehogs and foxes to safely drink, or for birds to get down to the shallow water to bathe, without fear of cats leaping on them out of the long grass. This means that to be a really effective wildlife habitat it needs a variety of different environments around it to cover all eventualities.

The value of your pond to wildlife in part will depend upon its surroundings. Giving your wildlife visitors the choice of dry or damp, cool or warm

Natural surroundings of pond

conditions nearby means that they can choose whatever they need for whichever activity is going on. So when making a decision about including a pond in your garden, it is important that you take all these factors into account if you want to provide the best wetland habitat possible.

An adjacent damp log pile, suitable for frogs and newts to hide in.

'This is fine!' - a Robin testing the waters

CHAPTER THREE
Pond Creation

Once you have decided that a pond habitat is for you, you should now stop and consider the safety aspects. If you have very young children visiting your garden you may need to think about whether a wildlife pond is the right thing for you, or whether the option of some other sort of wetland feature is a better choice, even for a limited time. If you are interested in encouraging more birds to your garden, a large terracotta or plastic plant pot saucer, topped up daily with fresh water for bathing and drinking, may suffice until your small human visitors are better able to cope with what could be a dangerous situation. An old-fashioned bird bath will not do much for your local frog population but it will provide fresh water for many species of bird until a proper wildlife pond is an option. Other alternatives such as bog gardens, mini-ponds and pebble ponds are a safe and easy means of introducing water to the garden and these are discussed in Chapter 7.

Protective netting over a pond isn't really a viable option for wildlife. Birds, frogs, toads and even hedgehogs can get tangled in netting, and access to the water for all wildlife is severely restricted. This also applies to a lesser extent to a metal grid over the water. If a proper

A wildlife mini-pond, perfect for a smaller garden

Pond Creation

Chaffinch drinking from a bird bath

A 'mini-pond' in a half barrel

Shallow marshy edges are an important habitat

Frogs will breed in a tiny pond

Mating Large Red Damselflies

Mammals such as foxes rely on garden ponds for drinking water

pond with open water is definitely for you, then it may be possible to construct it in a part of the garden that can temporarily be safely and securely fenced off to create a child-friendly feature. Access directly to the water for pond dipping or wildlife watching can then be supervised by an adult.

Choosing your site

Once you have given due consideration to the safety aspects and decided that a wildlife pond is for you, your next task is to decide on its location. This is not as easy as you may think as we have seen from the previous chapter just how important the surrounding habitats are. This means that you need to have space, not just for the pond but maybe for a little area of long grass somewhere beside it, or room to include a small bog garden. But don't let this put you off. Not much extra room is required – just enough to provide shelter for your emerging wildlife. And there may already be a place in the garden where your new pond can abut an existing 'wilder' place. However, don't neglect this requirement. The edges where habitats adjoin are very important, both in the wild and in your garden.

Next you must decide if you want your wildlife pond close to the house to enable you to see what's happening there or if the seclusion at the bottom of the garden is going to attract more wildlife. This is a difficult decision! I have partially solved this problem by creating several ponds of varying sizes in different situations. My small 'mini-pond' made in a half barrel is on a patio area outside the back door and is visible from several windows. This has a steady stream of birds bathing and drinking. A little further from the house is a medium-sized pond with plenty of shallow areas. This pond, known as the Marshy Pond, has frogs galore and plenty of damselflies breeding. An even larger pond (the Big Pond) has been created in a quiet part of the garden but is still visible from the house windows. This pond is where the local foxes come to drink, it has a

A really big wildlife pond is wonderful - if you have space!

Pond Creation

Some pond wildlife - a Great Crested Newt

Common Toad

Broad-bodied Chaser Dragonfly

Brown Hawker Dragonfly laying its eggs.

thriving population of Great Crested Newts and breeding Common Toads, and the big dragonflies species such as Broad-bodied Chaser, Brown Hawker and Emperor Dragonfly breed here. It attracts local ducks, especially Mallard, Grey Herons visit throughout the year and in the winter visiting Fieldfares bathe here. We are also fortunate to have that rarely seen native mammal, the Water Shrew, using this pond. This pond is surrounded by native rushes, plus Purple Loosestrife and Meadowsweet grow on the edges. A wildflower meadow bank has also been included on one side. It is a wild and very exciting place. I am fortunate to have a large garden where these wetland habitats and other small ponds and bog gardens can be made, but in an average garden a good compromise is a small wildlife pond away from the house and a bird drinking place – perhaps a bird bath, barrel pond or a water saucer – close to a window.

Don't forget that your pond will need topping up from time to time, so make sure you position it near a tap so that you can readily fill it with water as required. If you can, arrange for the rainwater overflow from the roof of a nearby building (even a garden shed) to keep the pond topped up as you will be creating a much cleaner environment for your wildlife visitors by utilising rainwater. This can be a permanent arrangement with a hose attached to the downpipe from the guttering of a shed or you may wish to attach a hose to a water butt tap when you want to top up the pond. With a more permanent set-up it is quite easy to dig the hose under the soil or lawn and arrange that the end emerges unobtrusively into a corner of the pond.

Lastly, when choosing the location of your pond, bear in mind that access may be an issue if you intend to hire a mini-digger to make the hole, although these will generally fit through the average garden gate.

Robin juvenile on small pond

Marginal Plants - Purple Loosestrife and ...

Grey Heron looking for a tasty morsel to eat

Ducks may visit larger garden ponds

... Meadowsweet on a pond edge

Sun or shade?

Next we must look at the garden's aspect and the amount of light it receives. It is usually recommended that ponds are placed in full sun, but I have had greatest success with ponds in conditions where they are shaded from the sun for at least a part of the day, either by a fence or maybe some tall shrubs. Every new pond will initially have a problem with blanket weed or other types of algae when it is first constructed, but one that is in full sun all day can take longer to reach that balance where the water is clear and sparkling. A pond in a very open spot will receive lots of light and heat from the sun and this will encourage the growth of all the plant life, including blanket weed. My Big Pond is shaded from the afternoon sun by a bank with trees and shrubs some distance away and only gets full sun in the morning and late afternoon. The water has always been beautifully clear and there is virtually no problem from a few leaves falling in. Similarly, a mini-pond in another part of my garden that is also slightly shaded by the house has never had a speck of blanket weed.

So, does this mean that a pond can be constructed under the shade of trees? The answer is yes, and I have created a wonderful 'Shady Pond' here in a small copse of trees and shrubs. This pond is very different from the others in that it does not attract large numbers of dragon- and damselflies which prefer to be in sunnier conditions, but it is still used daily by many birds drinking and bathing, plus it always has a few frogs sitting in the water in the spring and summer and toads hide amongst the damp logs lying around its edges. It is also used by a local fox as a drinking pool. If you only have a very shady spot available you can still go ahead with your pond, but it may not be a wildlife magnet. You can, however, plant ferns and other shade-loving plants around it and place logs on the edges to dip down into the water. You will still create a wonderfully cool, watery oasis, but don't expect quite as much in the way of visiting wildlife as you would in a more open situation. Having said that, this Shady Pond is one of my favourite places in my whole garden and it always attracts plenty of birds to watch and photograph.

Shady ponds are frequently used by toads...

... and frogs

A large pond in an open area but with some natural midday shade

The question of shade brings up another problem. Ponds under or near trees will undoubtedly accumulate leaves in the autumn. A few leaves falling into your pond will pose no great problem – they will sink to the bottom and as they break down will help to form a layer of mud where frogs may hibernate in the winter and flat worms, dragonfly larvae and many other creatures will live. Vast quantities of leaves falling into your pond will, however, decompose, causing a lack of oxygen in the water to the detriment of both plants and animals. In the winter, ice may form on the pond surface and trap gasses from decomposing vegetation which can over time change the ecology of your pond habitat completely. For more information on keeping your pond clean see Chapter 6 on Pond Maintenance.

Lastly, you may have problems excavating a pond under trees if there are extensive roots. You may even damage the roots and cause problems to mature trees or the tree roots may puncture a flexible pond liner. It is obviously an area that needs a lot of thought before you start.

So where does that leave us? My choice would always be a spot that was light and open and received plenty of sunlight for much of the day but, contrary to most advice, not out in full sun in the middle of a totally shade-free area. But somewhere in every garden there is a spot for even a tiny pond and, as far as wildlife is concerned, any water in the garden is better than no water at all.

There is one more important consideration when you are determining the site of your new pond. The flatter the area the easier it will be to level the edges, making the pond look natural and 'at home' in its surroundings. If you have a dip or hollow in the garden it may

A cool, watery oasis

be tempting to use this, but it will not necessarily be the best spot. Sometimes an area just above the dip (as long as it can be levelled in a satisfactory way) can create a very pleasing feature, with bog plants in the lowest lying area.

What type of lining?

There are basically four types of linings for ponds and these are outlined below, but for most situations only one is worth considering. Flexible pond liners made of butyl rubber or woven polythene are so versatile and inexpensive there is very little reason to consider anything else, even for really large ponds, unless you have excessively stony soil. As well as creating several ponds in my own garden, I have also been involved in the construction and planting of a pond with a very large surface area where a flexible liner was used to great effect, creating a large wetland habitat now full of life.

1. Concrete ponds

The pond in my parent's garden beside which I spent so much time was made of concrete because at that time there was no real alternative for a garden pond. Concrete, however, is rarely used today because of the many drawbacks associated with it. Firstly it is difficult to create a natural-looking pond using concrete, especially if you want grasses or other vegetation around the edges. The concrete itself may contain toxic substances which need to be locked in with a special sealant. In very cold weather, because of its rigid structure, a concrete pond may crack with the pressure of expanding ice on the surface and be very difficult to repair. All in all, concrete ponds are not wildlife friendly and hard work to construct as well.

2. Pre-formed fibreglass ponds

Most garden centres have a selection of these types of lightweight, preformed ponds in a range of shapes and sizes. Again, they have their drawbacks as the majority of them have a series of ledges around the edges to place plants but no gently sloping side to allow easy access to wildlife. It is also not easy to dig a hole that corresponds exactly to the shape of the preformed pond, which must be well supported underneath. Another drawback is that they are inclined to crack if they are full of ice in the winter. However, a preformed pond of this type could be useful as a bird drinking and bathing spot and indeed it is now possible to get these fibreglass structures especially for this purpose. These are designed to provide easy access to the water for birds, so a small one of this type may be a useful second watery habitat near the house.

3. Puddled clay ponds

As we have already seen, the majority of our 'wild' ponds in farmyards and also our network of canals were lined with clay. It is possible to buy clay for puddling and this may be an option if you already have a heavy clay soil in your garden. Creating a pond in this way is very hard work as the clay must be trodden with the feet to provide a smooth, continuous surface to line the hole you have prepared. This process is known as 'puddling' and the action of repeatedly treading on the wet clay modifies its structure causing the molecules to join together to create a watertight surface. Once a clay pond is filled with water it must never be allowed to dry out or the clay lining will shrink and crack and it is then difficult to repair. However, a puddled clay pond looks wonderfully natural, especially when surrounded with native reeds and aquatic flowering plants, and may be the choice for you. If you decide to try this method be sure to follow the manufacturer's recommendations for installation.

4. Flexible liners

The fourth option is the flexible liner which can be made from a variety of substances. The most expensive and longest lasting (usually with a manufacturer's 'lifetime' guarantee) is butyl rubber which will give you a natural-looking and easy to install pond. A cheaper option is woven polythene with a lifespan of about 30 years. Care must be taken with polythene to ensure that the edges are well covered as they may crack if exposed to sunlight for long periods.

Timing

Ponds can be created at almost any time of the year, but most people choose springtime to get started. Planting up your pond is best done in April or May, so it is a good idea to have your pond full of water and ready for your plants at this time. The alternative, and my personal preference, is to do the digging and lining in the late autumn. This allows your new pond to collect plenty of rainwater over the winter, which means that you will not need to fill it with tap water in the spring. You may also find that your local wildlife starts to use this new habitat that much earlier, even if there aren't any plants in it!

A pond created in the autumn will fill naturally with rainwater over the winter

Designing the shape

Choose a simple oval or kidney shape for a natural look

Once you have decided on the type of liner you wish to use, the position of the pond in the garden and your preferred time for creating your wetland habitat, you need to design the shape of the pond and dig the hole. One of the easiest ways to decide upon the best shape for your pond is to lay a hosepipe on the ground in an outline you like, roughly where you want the pond to be. Leave it for a day or two, go back to it from time to time to adjust the shape and over a few days you will slowly see just how your new feature will fit into your existing garden. Simple shapes are best, so a gentle oval or a curved kidney outline will look most natural. The beauty of the flexible liner is that it can be adapted to almost any shape, but the more complicated the outline, the harder it will be to disguise the liner and make the pond look natural.

Getting started with the digging

For a bigger pond you may need to hire digging equipment

Getting started

Now you need to start digging. If you have decided to create a large pond you may need to hire some sort of mini-digger. You also have to decide what you intend to do with the soil from the hole. The finished hole may look quite small, but you can guarantee that the pile of soil will be enormous! If you have no obvious way of using it, the best thing may be to hire a skip and remove it that way. If you are working on a relatively new garden you may be able to distribute the soil around the new borders, but do make sure that you save some soil to go back into the pond when you have put your liner in.

Low fertility soil from the hole can be used to create a wildflower bank

Making a meadow or creating a bank

The soil from the very bottom of the hole may be ideal for creating a wildflower meadow as it will usually be of low fertility. If you intend to create a meadow and a pond at the same time, spread some of the soil you excavate over the area where you envisage your meadow and allow it to settle before sowing with a native wildflower meadow seed mix in spring.

You could also use some of the soil to create a bank of some sort in the garden and this can produce a very useful wildlife habitat, particularly if it is south facing. Many ponds were created in the past with a 'rockery' beside them to make use of the excess soil from the hole, but these features look very unnatural in a wildlife garden. Instead you could sow a bank with seeds of

Bird's-foot Trefoil – a perfect wildflower for a sunny pond bank

low-growing native grasses and include wildflowers such as Bird's-foot Trefoil, Brooklime or Selfheal. You may wish to add the odd stone or rock here and there, pushed back into the soil to create shelter for slow worms or hibernation places for newts and toads.

A simple oval shape looks most natural when planted

Digging the hole

If your new pond is to be in existing grass, start by taking off the turf. This can be done with a spade or if the area is large you may want to hire a turf cutter. Place the turves to one side as they can be put to good use later.

Shapes with smooth outlines really do look best when creating a natural-looking pond. The simplest shape would be an oval with gently sloping sides, but it is essential to have a good proportion of deeper water to a depth of a minimum of 60 centimetres in the middle. It is best to avoid a shallow saucer shape as the large surface area will mean that evaporation and subsequent loss of water may be very rapid on hot days, so the deeper you can make your central portion the better. It will provide a reservoir of cool water for the creatures that prefer these conditions and the deepest area will be the best spot to plant a water lily. There will be somewhere safe for frogs (especially the males) to spend the winter without fear of freezing, and toads also do prefer a deeper pond, especially for breeding. A shallow pond will still be used by birds and mammals for drinking and bathing, but if you want a really good variety of wildlife breeding in your pond try to create a deep middle section.

You can of course make the pond profile in whatever shape you wish as long as it has at least one gently sloping side, but the more complicated the shape the harder it is to dig and make a neat job of the liner. I tend to favour a gently sloping edge around about one quarter to one third of the pond perimeter. This slope can be covered with pebbles if you wish to provide safe access to wildlife. A ledge of 20 to 30 centimetres depth around the rest of the pond gives a secure flat place to establish marginal plants without compromising the accessibility of the water to wildlife.

Excavate the hole to a depth of about 15 centimetres deeper all over than you would like the finished pond to be. This allows for the next stage of protecting the liner and for your planting medium to be placed on top of the liner. As you dig, try to ensure that the edges are level all round. This can be done by placing a plank of wood across the pond with a spirit level on top. If the sides are not level, you will tend to get ugly bits of exposed liner on the higher side above the water level, which may be hard to disguise with marginal plants.

Pond Creation

Protect the liner with sand or underlay

Once the hole is the size and shape you want, and it will take a bit of adjusting here and there to get it right, you need to make sure that your liner is not going to get punctured by any sharp objects underneath it. Go over the exposed soil very thoroughly and remove any bits of sharp stone, old crockery, glass or sticks that may be in the soil. To protect your liner further, line the hole with about 5 centimetres of fine sand. For a really professional job you can buy material especially for this purpose. I think it is well worth investing a little extra in this liner underlay as your pond will be such an important feature in your wildlife garden. If you have very stony soil the underlay could be really essential.

Once you have dug and shaped the hole you now need to measure it before you buy your liner. The chances are that you will already have thought about how much liner you need, but do delay ordering or buying it until you are completely happy with the pond shape and size. It is very easy to get carried away and dig a bigger hole than you originally intended only to find that the liner you have bought is too small! It is difficult, and annoying, to have to fill in part of the hole you have just worked hard to dig out!

Measuring up for the liner

There is an easy formula to work out how much liner you need. Measure the length and the width of the hole you have dug and then the deepest part — the depth you have created. To calculate the length of liner, you need to add twice the depth measurement to the length of your hole and then add on another metre for the overlap on the edges. Repeat this for the width — add twice the depth to the width measurement plus one metre.

A large pond with an expensive liner will benefit from underlay to protect it from punctures

This will give you the length and width you need to order. Liners are available in all shapes and sizes from many garden centres or by mail order online, and manufacturers and suppliers can provide a liner of any size by joining pieces for you if necessary to produce the required size.

Lining the pond

Once you are completely happy with the shape and size of your pond and have lined your empty hole with some underlay or other soft material, you are ready to put in the liner. Open it out carefully, get a friend or two to help you carry it to the hole and simply drape it over. Adjust it until you have an even overlap all the way around the hole and hold down the edges with smooth stones or bricks.

You now have a choice. The manufacturer's instructions will probably recommend that you start to fill the pond and allow the weight of the water to gently pull the liner down into the hole. This method works well if you are not intending to backfill the pond with soil, but a good wildlife pond should have about 10 centimetres of soil over the liner in which to grow aquatic plants. It is much easier with this type of natural-looking pond to ease the liner into the hole at this stage before any water goes in, slowly releasing the stones around the edge a little at a time and gently pleating any excess liner here and there until the liner is settled into the hole. If the pond is a simple shape, this will be very easy to do. If you want to let the liner ease down as the pond fills, you will need

Large pond with underlay and liner, ready for a covering of soil for planting

to throw the soil in later, which can be very messy.

Once the liner is settled into the hole you can start to distribute the soil you have saved evenly over it to a depth of about 10 centimetres. Try not to walk on the liner whatever it is made of, although butyl will take some weight. If your pond is large and you need to get into the hole to distribute the soil, take your shoes off before you walk on it – you really don't want to make a hole in it with walking boots! For smaller ponds it is easier to lie on your stomach at the edge to spread the soil out, or simply throw it in a spade at a time.

If you have made a ledge somewhere, now is the time to make use of the turf you saved. The turves, turned upside down, make a good planting medium for marginal plants and can be laid along the ledges with the grassy side down. The vegetation soon dies off once it is under the water, and the soil and matted roots of the grass hold together well for planting marginals. If you don't have turf, simply place a layer of stone-free soil on the ledges.

If you are making a sloping pebble area, now is the time to place the pebbles carefully on the slope, preferably without soil beneath them. This will ensure that the beach is kept relatively open and will not be quickly colonised by plants, ensuring easy access to the water. When you are happy with the result you can start to fill the pond.

Filling the pond

Obviously the quality of the water you put into your pond is very important. If you have created your habitat in the autumn it should fill up with rainwater quite quickly and might already have a few birds bathing on the sloping edges and possibly a few frogs or toads in the water. If you are creating your pond in the spring however, you may have no choice but to use tap water to fill it. If you can in any way use some stored rainwater from a water butt, or you have managed to arrange for rainwater to drain into the pond from a nearby roof, it will start the pond off on the right footing.

Having to use tap water is not a disaster, but it may contain chemicals that we would prefer not to have in a

Sloping edges create a natural effect when planted

Pond Creation

Gently fill the pond or allow rainwater to fill it naturally

Stones and logs can be added to create a natural-looking edge

A few months later - the pond begins to settle naturally into the garden

wildlife pond. Chlorine will evaporate after a few days, but there might be traces of heavy metals, pesticides or other compounds which could potentially be harmful to aquatic life. Most importantly though, tap water often contains nitrates and phosphates from fertilizers added to countryside crops and these will remain in the water until they are used up by your plants. This is potentially a problem – in particular it can encourage the rapid growth of various aquatic algae in the first few weeks, but once you understand what is happening it need not be an issue. Chapter 4 on Planting Your Pond explains how to minimize the problems caused by blanket weed and other aquatic algae.

If you are using a hose pipe and tap water, trickle the water slowly and gently onto a few upturned turves in the deepest part of the pond to stop the soil layer getting too stirred up. It will look messy at first but it doesn't take long for everything to settle.

Gently fill the pond right up to the top (which may take longer than you think) and then sit back and admire your handiwork. The chances are you are looking at a messy, muddy water hole with scum floating on the top! Don't worry. All ponds look like this when the water first goes in. Go away and have a cup of tea, and by the time you return there will probably be a bird or two having a drink or, as happened with the first wildlife pond I made, there may already be dragonflies hawking over the water surface, checking out this new habitat. At this point, leave the pond alone for a few days to settle down.

The habitat edges

Your next job will be to work on the pond edges to create a natural-looking transition between the water and the surrounding habitat. The most common mistake with wildlife ponds is made at this point. Be aware that if you lay turf up to the edge and down into the water, your water level will drop rapidly as water automatically wicks up through the turf (or indeed the soil) and evaporates. See the section on Bog Gardens in Chapter 7 for more information on this. The trick here is to have a small break at the water's edge between the soil covering the pond liner and the grass or soil at the pond edge. This break is easier to maintain and hide with good planting if your pond has a shallow ledge. I know many people who have created the perfect looking 'natural' pond in this way with turf positioned right up to and over the edges into the water only to find that it has virtually emptied overnight because of this wicking effect.

Once you have filled your pond and created your natural-looking edges, you can think about planting.

Edges planted with Bugle and Primroses - a 'natural' pond in light shade

Lady's Smock or Cuckoo Flower on a pond edge

CHAPTER FOUR
Planting your Pond

Planting up your pond really is the fun bit and my preference is to plant in spring. If you have completed your pond construction in March or April you can get to work planting as soon as the water has settled down which generally takes three or four days. If your pond was created in the autumn and then left to fill naturally with rainwater, it will have had plenty of time through the winter to settle without too much input from you, so spring planting is again the best option. Most garden centres and plant nurseries stock aquatic plants throughout the year now, so with a pond constructed in autumn you may be tempted to begin your planting as soon as you have finished, but my preference would always be to establish plants between late March and May. This is the time of year when they really get growing.

Firstly though, some advice about pond algae. It is very common, practically normal in fact, to find that a new pond develops green water very quickly after filling. Many people are very concerned about this and attempt to put the situation right by removing some of the green water and replacing it with 'clean' tap water. A couple of days later the pond is a vivid shade of green again. Alternatively chemicals may be used which might cure the problem in the short term but can damage other plants if the amount of chemical used is not calculated accurately. A wildlife pond should be as free of chemicals as possible.

Several algal species may find a home in your new pond

It is quite important and very useful to understand what is happening here as understanding the processes involved will make an algal problem easier to deal with. Green water contains tiny single-celled algae which are all around us – in the water you have filled your pond with, in the soil in the garden, even in the air. These are tiny plants that thrive on nutrients in water and, by adding more tap water containing nitrates and phosphates, you have just provided the perfect conditions for their growth and multiplication. Once they are in the water in your pond, they will grow and increase until their green colour becomes visible in the form of a green soup! However, they are actually doing something very useful. They are using up the excess nutrients in the pond water, making a more balanced environment. As we have already seen, tap water may contain nitrates, phosphates and other chemicals, washed into our water supply from fertilised fields. A new pond filled with tap water will therefore have a greater problem with these tiny plants than one filled with rainwater. If you remove some of the water and replace it with more tap water, you are simply adding more nutrients – feeding the algal plants in effect – so they will flourish afresh. All aquatic plants remove nitrogen from pond water as they grow, but these tiny algae do it more rapidly and efficiently than almost anything else. The good news though is that once they have used up the excess nitrogen they will quickly disappear, sometimes overnight, and the water will look fresh and clear. If excess algal growth continues to be a problem see Chapter 6 on Pond Maintenance.

Excess nitrogen can get into pond water in other ways, from decomposing leaves or plants for instance, or from fish in the pond producing nitrogen in their faeces. Keeping a balance of nutrients in the water is something we want to try to achieve. The aquatic plants you are about to add to your pond will help to set up this balance. They will clean and purify the water by using up the excess nutrients, supply hiding places for your wildlife, shade the water surface to keep it cool and provide food for many of the creatures you hope will take up residence.

Natives or non-natives

Every wildlife pond should have some native wildflowers and my personal preference is to use entirely native

A small pond planted with native wildflowers

Planting your Pond

plants in a wildlife pond habitat. We are fortunate to have a wealth of beautiful wetland plants at our disposal for all areas of a pond and this is the perfect opportunity to give some of them pride of place in your garden, but there is no harm in including one or two of your favourite non-natives if you wish. Firstly though, check that they are not plants known to cause problems if they escape into our native waterways. All aquatic plants should be chosen carefully – many will grow exceptionally quickly in these ideal conditions – and, of course, they should never be taken from the wild, which is illegal. The list of wetland wildflowers on page 49 will give you some ideas about which ones are particularly suitable for garden ponds.

Sources of plants

British native plants, such as Bogbean, Water Mint and Water Violet, can be found now in many garden centres in their water plant section. In garden centres though, they may be rather expensive compared with plant nurseries that specialise in aquatics of this sort. Check the suppliers at the end of this book for aquatic plant nurseries offering a mail order service.

A tempting alternative would be to obtain plants from a friend or neighbour's pond, but be sure you know what you are getting. At all costs avoid anything that might be a non-native invasive species and if in any doubt go to a specialist supplier for your plants. One advantage of obtaining plants from a friend though is that you will inevitably get some aquatic creepy crawlies into the bargain – a good start for your wildlife pond. As most pond plants grow very quickly, we all need to thin them out from time to

Bogbean

Water Mint with a visiting Small Copper butterfly

Planting your Pond

Water Snails are vital to a healthy pond

Rushes and sedges create a natural pond edge

time and the excess generally goes onto the compost heap. I would much rather pass these onto a friend starting up a new pond if I can. Oxygenators in particular can grow exceptionally quickly, and these usually have the eggs of water snails on them or small damselfly larvae clinging to the leaves.

Types of plants

Of all the types of plant we can grow in our gardens, pond plants are perhaps the most rewarding. We have already seen that in the right conditions they will grow rapidly and make your pond look mature and inviting within a few months. Many also have the advantage of adapting to a range of conditions, from damp soil to several centimetres of water on the pond ledge. In general though, pond plants are divided into the different categories listed below and a well-stocked pond will have a few of each type.

1. Emergents

These are very important plants in the pond as they are rooted well below water level but have their leaves above water level. This means that they are available for creatures such as the larvae of dragonflies to easily leave their watery habitat when they are ready to transform into beautiful winged adults. The larvae will crawl up the plant leaves, preferring species with smooth, sword-shaped leaves, out of the

Empty dragonfly larval cases after hatching

Planting your Pond

Providing shade - Brandy Bottle and ...

... our native White Water Lily

water and into the air, where they will complete their transformation. Good examples of emergent plants are the rushes and sedges, Branched Bur-reed, Flowering Rush and Yellow Iris, also known as Yellow Flag. Emergent plants will thrive on the pond ledge or in areas of the pond where the water is relatively shallow.

2. Floaters

Plants with floating leaves are very important in your pond as they provide shade on the water during warm, sunny weather. They will help to keep the pond water cool and help to prevent the spread of blanket weed and other algae. Any plant with floating leaves, however small, will perform this function, but water lilies are the most useful

Yellow Iris or Flag

Fringed Water Lily

45

Duckweed helps to maintain cool water

Water Mint

Brooklime

Lesser Spearwort

Marsh Marigold

ally in shading the water. This is a good opportunity to use a non-native plant if you wish. The native White Water Lily has the potential to become a very large plant and is therefore not really suitable for a small pond, so choose a smaller non-native if you would like a lily. Other good water-shading native plants are Fringed Water Lily, Duckweed and Frogbit. Aim to have at least 30 per cent of the water surface covered with floating plant leaves in the summer. Floaters such as lilies should be planted into the deepest part of the pond.

3. Marginals

These are the really adaptable plants that will often grow in damp soil as well as on the pond ledge. They provide a very important habitat for wildlife around the margins of the pond as well as giving it a natural look by hiding the liner if the water level drops. Many of our native wetland plants are marginals and include colourful species such as Water Mint, Brooklime, Lesser Spearwort and Marsh Marigold. Some marginals can also be classed as emergents (Yellow Flag for example) and many will also grow in boggy conditions.

4. Oxygenators

Oxygenating plants are crucial in your new pond which will not thrive without them. They provide the oxygen upon which your pond wildlife depends. If you can possibly find a source of native oxygenators then do use them. They will generally grow less quickly than non-natives which can be very invasive, but they will provide a better home for the small aquatic creatures that find their way into your pond. However, if non-natives are all that is available to you these will perform perfectly well but they do need to be selected with care as many are invasive and some positively harmful. Choose carefully and make sure that you avoid those species listed on page 49. Oxygenators should be placed in the deeper water.

If natives are not available, Canadian Pondweed (*Elodea canadensis*) is a good oxygenator and can be kept under control, but make sure it does not 'escape' into natural aquatic habitats.

Oxygenating plants are essential to the health of your pond

Purple Loosestrife

5. Bog plants

The term 'bog plant' refers to those species which prefer a soil that *never* dries out completely and includes some of our most colourful wildflowers. Purple Loosestrife, Ragged Robin, Bugle and Lady's Smock are all attractive examples of native bog plants. If you are not planning a separate bog garden you may be able to include some of these species around the shallow pond margins. Be aware though that the edges of garden ponds can actually be very dry, but the ledge, if

Ragged Robin

you have constructed one, may be too wet. A gently sloping edge may be the best spot for some bog-loving species which will adapt and find their preferred water depth by self seeding or spreading by runners. Don't forget though to keep some of your gentle slope completely free of plants to provide easy access for bathing birds or drinking hedgehogs.

Bugle

Lady's Smock visited by Orangetip butterfly

Inevitably all these different types of wetland plant will seed and spread around the pond until they find a place where they are happy, but it is a good idea to at least start off with a few of each kind.

How to plant

One of the most attractive features of a good wildlife pond is its natural look, and this is achieved by planting your aquatic plants directly into the soil covering your liner rather than in containers. If you have placed inverted turf on a pond ledge, this is a perfect planting medium for marginals and emergents. The general idea though is to take the plants out of their pots and push the whole rootball into the mud or turf. Some plants may want to float back up to the surface at this point. If so, anchor them down with a large stone propped onto the rootball – it can be removed when the plant has established a root system in the mud which happens very quickly. Plants such as lilies for deeper water should be carefully removed from the pot or planting basket they arrive in and the rootball wrapped in a piece of hessian. Tie the hessian gently around the plant stem to keep the whole thing together and then, as gently as possible, throw the plant into the deepest area of water. I have never found it necessary to lower lilies into the water to allow the leaf stems to extend over a few days as is often recommended. They always seem to have survived this rather brutal introduction to their new home and leaves very quickly appear

Planting your Pond

on the water surface. If, however, you are creating your pond in springtime you may prefer to place the lilies in position as the pond is being filled.

This natural way of planting up your pond will give your pond wildlife lots of vegetation in which to live and thrive. There are some plants that are just too vigorous for small garden ponds and should be planted with caution. They could be introduced to your pond in conventional planting baskets, but bear in mind that plants can escape from baskets over time. These plants are marked as suitable for very large ponds only in the table on page 78.

Oxygenators also need to be planted – only a few survive by floating around in the water. Push the cut or rooted ends into the soil in the deepest water you can safely reach or add them to the pond soil as your new pond is filling with water.

Native oxygenators
Curly Pondweed *Potamogeton crispus*
Hornwort *Ceratophyllum demersum*
Spiked Water Milfoil *Myriophyllum spicatum*
Water Starwort *Callitriche* ssp.

Avoid at all costs!
There are a few non-native plants (particularly oxygenators) that are causing enormous ecological problems in our native wetland areas. These have generally escaped from garden ponds or have been dumped by unsuspecting gardeners. They are dangerously invasive, threatening these precious natural habitats. Do not plant the following under any circumstances:

Non-native plants to avoid
Alien Marsh Pennywort *Hydrocotyle ranunculoides*
Curly Waterweed *Lagarosiphon major*
New Zealand Pygmyweed *Crassula helmsii*
Nuttall's Pondweed *Elodea nuttallii*
Parrots Feather *Myriophyllum aquaticum*
Water Fern *Azolla filiculoides*

If you have any of these plants in an existing pond, contact your local Wildlife Trust for advice about disposing of them. NEVER dump them in the countryside, particularly not in wetland habitats. Most plants will break down naturally on the compost heap, especially if they are chopped up first. Hopefully these plants will soon no longer be found for sale in nurseries and garden centres.

Azure Damselfly

CHAPTER FIVE
Pond Wildlife

Perhaps the most exciting thing about a wildlife pond is that you hardly need to do anything, except add water, to attract a wide variety of wildlife. Dragonflies, water beetles, water boatmen, pond skaters, in fact many fascinating insects will investigate a new pond on day one if they are in your area, even before you have added plants. If you plant up your pond thoughtfully though, a huge range of aquatic life will make use of the water to live and breed, or simply to drink and bathe. And you don't have to introduce your wildlife – everything will find this new habitat without any help.

We have seen how important the construction of a pond can be, especially in terms of its accessibility to wildlife. If you already have a garden pond that is not particularly wildlife friendly in terms of easy access to the water, Chapter 7 has some ideas on adapting an existing pond to make it a better habitat for wildlife.

To a certain extent, the size, shape and depth of your new pond will determine the type of creatures that will use it, as will the habitat around it. But the average garden pond is quite capable of attracting a wide range of wildlife including frogs and Common Newts, several dragonfly and damselfly species, water snails, boatmen, beetles and pond skaters as well as many other smaller aquatic insects. In addition, birds of all shapes and sizes will visit even a tiny pond. Hedgehogs and foxes will drink

Common Newt chasing the larva of a diving beetle, *Acilius sulcatus*.

Whirligig Beetles

Common Frog

51

Pond Wildlife

Water Snail

Pond Skater

Common Toad

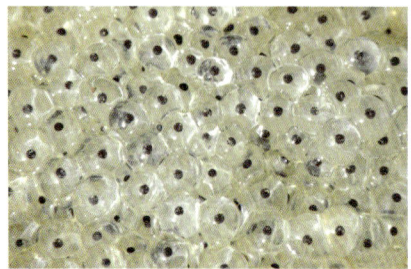

Jelly-like blobs of frog spawn

Large Red Damselfly

Spawning frogs

Strings of toad spawn

from the smallest saucer pond. So what wildlife can we reasonably expect in an average garden pond?

Amphibians

Frogs, toads and newts use our ponds for breeding in springtime but spend much of the rest of the year in the surrounding habitat – hence the importance of getting that right when your pond is constructed. Spawning of frogs can start as early as January in the south of England, toads spawn a little later, usually in March or April and newts latest of all (April or May), but the breeding of all these amphibians is dependent on temperatures and weather conditions.

The Common Frog is the most likely amphibian to use a garden pond for breeding – indeed there are thought to be more Common Frogs in suburban areas now than in the countryside. They are not particularly fussy about the type of pond they use and generally lay their jelly-like blobs of spawn in the relatively warm and shallow water close to the pond edge. Common Toads lay their spawn in long strings like transparent necklaces, with the black eggs visible along the length, and they wind the spawn around aquatic plants. In general, toads prefer a pond with a good deep area of cool water, and sometimes frogs and toads won't cohabit in the same pond. The Common Newt, also known as the Smooth Newt, will find its way into even the smallest pond. They lay their eggs singly and attach each one to the undersides of aquatic plant leaves in a pond, especially the oxygenators. The eggs are tiny and usually very difficult to see. Great Crested Newts will also use a garden pond, but this declining amphibian does not have a regular distribution in Britain and is a protected species. I have been fortunate to have had these amphibians both in my former garden in Oxfordshire and in my current one in South Shropshire where my large wildlife pond has a good population of these beautiful and fascinating amphibians. Great

Mating Common Toads

Great Crested Newt

53

Pond Wildlife

Crested Newts are almost black and quite large – they can reach up to 18 centimetres in length – so they can be distinguished by size and colour from Common Newts which are usually a muddy brown. Great Crested Newts are fully protected by law under the Wildlife and Countryside Act 1981 and their habitat should not be disturbed in any way. If they are locally common in your area they will happily cohabit with Smooth Newts, but it is worth remembering that they will eat the spawn and tadpoles of Common Frogs which may deplete your population of these amphibians.

If amphibians of any species are around in your area they will soon find a new pond and make it their home. Importing frogspawn from other ponds is an easy way to spread disease and is best avoided.

Reptiles

The only native reptile likely to use a garden pond is the Grass Snake. They are particularly attracted to water, love to swim, and frogs make up a major part of their diet. Again they are a protected species and the habitat around your pond will be important if you want to attract this reptile. Compost heaps are favourite breeding places for Grass Snakes.

Larger insects

Many winged insects breed in water, and dragon- and damselflies are favourites with many people. The size of your pond and the depth of the water is significant when attracting dragonflies as the larger species, especially the beautiful green female Emperor Dragonfly, prefer a big pond. Dragonfly larvae may spend many months in the water, although the

Grass Snake

Female Emperor Dragonfly egg-laying

Pond Wildlife

length of time depends on the species and also on weather conditions. They feed on the smaller creatures in the silt layers at the bottom of the water. Dragonflies are also dependent on the habitat surrounding your pond as, like their aquatic larvae, the adults also feed on the smaller insects they can hunt and catch around the garden. The pond plants on the water margins are also very important for dragonflies as these enable the larvae to emerge when they are ready to leave the water in spring and early summer. These plants also provide perching places from which the adults hunt or 'hawk' and they will often return to the same spot with their prey. In our countryside many of our native dragon- and damselfly species are declining due to destruction of their habitat and a lack of small insects on which they feed, so garden ponds can be havens for many species.

Water boatmen, water beetles and pond skaters are some of the more visible insects that inhabit a garden pond. Many people have concerns about the larvae of mosquitoes, midges or gnats that breed in water, but in general these are never a problem in a well-balanced pond. The vast majority will provide food for frog and newt tadpoles or other carnivorous insects such as the Great Diving Beetle, which can even catch and eat small fish!

Water boatman

Common Blue Damselfly

Adult dragonflies hunt or 'hawk' from a prominent place

55

Smaller Animals

A well-balanced pond will soon attract a wide range of the smaller aquatic animals that inhabit water at some point during their life cycles. All have important roles in a wildlife pond. *Daphnia*, sometimes called water fleas, and other small aquatic invertebrates provide food for the larger creatures, and water snails are important for keeping the water clean and fresh. Encourage all that comes as it will have its place in the overall scheme of things and in the food chain in the garden as a whole. Swallows, Swifts and House Martins, as well as bats rely on the small winged insects that hatch from the pond over the summer months. To find out more about the smaller creatures and the roles they perform, get a good identification book on the subject and indulge in a bit of pond dipping.

Swallows benefit from a garden pond

Mammals

The importance of water to mammals that come to the garden has already been mentioned. Hedgehogs and foxes in particular will drink at a wildlife pond, provided the access is easy and safe; in my Oxfordshire garden Muntjac and Roe Deer were occasional visitors.

Birds

All birds need to drink and bathe, and some species need to visit water more frequently than others. Finches in particular have a very dry diet as they eat mainly seeds and appear to need to visit fresh water very regularly. Goldfinches, Chaffinches, Greenfinches and Linnets are frequent and very welcome visitors to my garden ponds. If you have chosen to provide a bird bath, a drinking dish or 'mini-pond' rather than a large wildlife pond you can still expect a wide range of your local bird species to make use of the water to bathe as well as drink.

Greenfinch drinking from a mini-pond

Pond Wildlife

Male Great-spotted Woodpecker drinking

A Chiffchaff bathing

One of my tiny 'barrel ponds', situated right outside my back door, attracts many common bird species to drink and bathe, including tits, House Sparrows, Great-spotted Woodpeckers and various finches, while less common garden visitors, such as Grey Wagtails, Chiffchaffs and Whitethroats, also use it from time to time. My larger pond often has a couple of Mallard visiting on quiet evenings, Grey Herons are regular visitors and even the local Buzzards and Kestrels will come to drink.

Fish

In general, fish and wildlife ponds do not mix well. Koi Carp or Goldfish are much better off in ponds on their own as they will quickly devour spawn and tadpoles, thus preventing the build-up of a population of frogs, toads and newts. They also excrete nitrogen into the water which can aggravate a problem with blanket weed and other algae. If you enjoy having fish in your pond, native sticklebacks are fascinating and can breed well in garden ponds once established, but they are very aggressive little fish and their diet consists of many of the other small creatures living in your wildlife pond.

Predators

Grey Herons can be a problem in garden ponds but generally only in ponds stocked with fish. Herons will also eat frogs and toads, so do expect to see them from time to time, even if your pond is small. If they really are eating everything in your new habitat,

Many larger bird species like this Kestrel will drink from a garden pond

do not be tempted to place a fake 'heron' beside the pond to deter the real thing as this is more likely to encourage another heron to join in! These birds are quite often seen fishing in groups, so the sight of a 'heron' at your pond edge may well alert another bird to the possibility of available food. The best deterrent is a strand of thin string about 20 centimetres high around the edge of the pond. Herons tend to alight at a pond edge and then walk into the shallow water. A strand of string deters them when they brush it with their legs. Alternatively, try to appreciate this graceful native bird and make sure that your frogs and toads have plenty of cover to hide in the form of aquatic plants of all kinds, but especially those with floating leaves.

Wildlife and the Law

Some species of native aquatic wildlife, especially Great Crested Newts, have special protection in law because of their decline in the countryside. There is also legislation governing the introduction of many species to garden ponds, and handling of some plants or amphibians may require a licence. Similarly, the release of plants or animals (especially exotic species such as terrapins or bullfrogs) in an unauthorized place is against the law. If you are in any doubt about any of these issues contact your local Wildlife Trust or the Environment Agency.

A wildlife pond should be free of ornamental fish

A complete wildlife pond habitat with undisturbed edges

Duckweed is a very valuable plant for a wildlife pond

CHAPTER SIX
Pond Maintenance

Taking care of your pond to maximise its wildlife potential and keep it looking attractive and healthy is something that requires a gentle touch. After construction, it would be possible to do nothing at all and to create a wonderful wildlife paradise for a couple of years. But neglecting maintenance means that the pond habitat with its open water will slowly change as it evolves naturally into a bog. This is still a useful wildlife habitat but is not what we are trying to achieve in a garden situation. On the other hand, a pond that is continually cleaned, disturbed and interfered with may look sparkling and pretty but will not be suitable for those species that prefer an undisturbed habitat.

The answer here is to do as little as possible while still maintaining a habitat with plenty of open water between a good covering of plants. Below are some of the maintenance jobs that may need to be done on a seasonal basis.

Spring and summer
These are the seasons to leave everything alone as much as possible. It is sometimes suggested that excess Duckweed is removed from a pond in the springtime, but this is when floating plants are particularly valuable as a means of keeping frog and toad tadpoles safe from predators, plus this is a plant that shades the water keeping it cool and algae free. Only remove plants at this time if they are particularly overgrown and threatening to close up all the open water, and even then do this using extreme caution. Remember that newt eggs are laid individually onto the leaves of oxygenators and other plants, so do not thin these out at all at this time.

Throughout spring and summer make sure that your pond is topped up little and often. If you have been able to arrange the rainwater overflow from a roof or a water butt to drain into your pond, topping up may be only an occasional job, depending on the weather. If you are reliant on tap water however, a little now and again will help to avoid the problem of quantities of nitrates or other undesirable chemicals entering the habitat in one go.

Rainwater overflow from a shed roof

61

If blanket weed is an issue at this time of year, try adding a bundle of barley straw which is thought to produce a natural compound that inhibits the growth of algae. However check carefully when buying these products in garden centres as some are impregnated with a chemical algaecide which could be detrimental to plants in your pond.

Autumn

Autumn is the time to remove excess plant growth, but this job should still be done with extreme care. By the autumn the larger animals – frogs, newts and toads – will have left the water. Frogs, especially the males, may return to hibernate in the mud at the bottom of your pond as the weather gets colder, so if you are doing any cleaning work, October is the best month for this job. Plants such as Duckweed and oxygenating plants can be removed gently with a rake. Take great care not to scrape the bottom of your pond! Liners can be easily damaged and, although they are repairable, there is nothing worse than finding your pond empty the day after a clean-out (as I have) and it could take a long time for the wildlife to recover.

Plants removed in this way should be left overnight or even longer on the pond side to allow any aquatic wildlife in amongst the leaves to crawl out back into the water. You will be amazed at the number of small dragon- and damselfly larvae, water snails and other

An overgrown pond in need of careful maintenance

tiny aquatic creatures living in this vegetation. You can help the process if you wish by sorting through the plants and collecting the larvae and other creatures you find, but in general it is easier to allow them to make their own way back into the water. Once you are fairly sure there is nothing left, these excess plants can be put on the compost heap.

Usually it is only rapidly growing plants such as oxygenators that need this treatment, but every couple of years you may need to reduce the volume of some of the marginals and deeper water plants. If you have been careful not to plant the really rampant species mentioned in Chapter 4 and on page 78 you should be able to do this without creating too much disturbance. Plants such as Fringed Water Lily, Water Mint and Bogbean spread by runners and can generally be uprooted from the mud at the bottom of the pond fairly easily. Others like Cyperus Sedge, Purple Loosestrife or Gipsywort seed freely in shallow water and will need to be loosened from the mud and removed to the compost heap. Any plants in containers can also be dealt with at this time of year. Lift the container from the water, gently dislodge the plant and split the root by hand or with a sharp knife. Repot the section you want to retain, covering the soil around the plant roots with a layer of gravel to prevent the compost from floating out when the container goes back into the water.

Bogbean spreads rapidly and may need keeping in check

The other important autumn task is the removal of excessive quantities of leaves from the pond. A few leaves falling into your pond will not matter greatly, but large quantities will break down and increase the nutrient levels, creating problems later with the growth of blanket weed and other species of algae. Leaves can also cause a problem as they decompose over the winter months. They produce toxic gasses such as methane during decomposition. This, when trapped under a frozen pond surface, may affect the survival of frogs and other creatures spending the winter months in the depths of the pond. If you have large quantities of leaves in your garden they should be gently raked from the pond surface on a regular basis through the autumn.

Netting a pond to catch leaves is not a good option as many creatures become entangled or trapped.

Winter

During the winter months, your pond may look lifeless, but a great many creatures are resting under the water surface and your concern at this time is to ensure that they survive the cold weather. If you have constructed the pond with a depth of at least 60 centimetres, most creatures will safely pass the winter months in the deepest part of the pond, but a covering of ice can affect their chances of survival. The safest and most effective way of clearing a 'breathing hole' for your pond is by using a small metal saucepan of very hot water. Simply hold the base

Foxes and other mammals may depend on the water in your pond

In the winter ice on the pond surface may need to be dealt with gently

of the saucepan on the ice surface and let the heat slowly melt a circle of ice. This will effectively open up a space, allowing gasses to escape without greatly disturbing the wildlife beneath the surface. It is not advisable to pour hot water onto the ice or to break a hole in it. Both these actions are thought to produce a 'shock' effect in the water, potentially detrimental to the wildlife therein.

Repairing leaks

Most flexible pond liners with leaks can be repaired by using a kit from a pond liner manufacturer or a garden centre. These are very effective but they do rely on the liner surface being completely dry. If your liner has been torn, either by careless use of a rake or some other accidental damage, allow the water to leak out until it maintains its level. The hole will be somewhere on this level. It will then be necessary to manually remove a little more water until the tear is completely exposed and can be effectively dried. Follow the repair kit instructions and be prepared to repeat the operation! It generally works in the end but not necessarily first time. If your pond has sprung a leak halfway down or more, try to repair it as soon as possible regardless of the time of year. A pond that empties due to a tear in the liner will be of little use to the wildlife inhabiting it if the water disappears completely. If the leak is nearer the surface, try to keep the pond well topped up until the autumn which is the best time for repair.

Wildlife ponds can look very beautiful in the winter months

Removing a build-up of silt

Again choose the autumn for this job. If your pond has accumulated so much silt that the depth of water is greatly reduced, it will be necessary to remove some of it before it becomes a bog garden. You may decide to remove some of the water or to attempt the job, particularly if your pond is small, by leaning in and scooping out some of the sludge with a smooth-edged receptacle such as a plastic food container. Equip yourself with a large sheet of polythene spread out at the pond side and begin by heaping up the surface layer of silt here. This can be reintroduced to the pond (it will contain vast numbers of useful creepy crawlies and bacteria) once the sludge from the very bottom has been taken out and put on the compost heap. However you perform this messy task, keep all sharp tools away from the pond liner!

Renovating your pond completely

This is a job to avoid at all costs if you can. By cleaning out a pond completely, you could destroy a habitat that has been built up over many months or even years. Keeping your pond maintained at a low but continuous level throughout its life avoids such drastic action. If you have Great Crested Newts in your pond you will be breaking the law by causing such disturbance.

Long grass near your pond is likely to be sheltering wildlife

If you are sure that you do not have newts and need, for whatever reason, to reconstruct your pond, you must have an alternative nearby to hold the creatures you will find. Fill an old bath or other container with water from the pond (not fresh tap water), add as many plants, particularly oxygenators, as you can and carefully transfer any creatures as you find them. Return them to the new or refurbished pond as soon as you can.

Maintenance of the area around your pond

We have already seen how the habitat *around* your pond is of great importance. Take great care when mowing long grass near a pond and avoid disturbance of log piles and other habitats when you are carrying out work nearby. There may be newts, toads, and even Grass Snakes residing there. Any long grass near your pond could be carefully cut on a rotational basis to ensure that there is always somewhere for your wildlife to live in safety.

In conclusion, try to do a little regular pond maintenance every autumn rather than leave the jobs to pile up. The fewer disturbances you create to the pond habitat, the happier your wildlife will be.

A meadow habitat close to a small pond

A terracotta plant saucer

A small barrel pond with a log habitat nearby

CHAPTER SEVEN
Pond Alternatives

Water is vital to wildlife. Some creatures would not be in your garden at all if it wasn't for their daily visit to the water you are providing. Others such as frogs, toads, newts, dragon- and damselflies rely on water for breeding and thus maintaining their populations. Many smaller creatures live their whole lives in aquatic habitats and we have seen that by providing a source of water that you could be contributing to the conservation of many species that are declining in the countryside. But a pond is not suitable for every garden for a variety of reasons and therefore alternative ways of providing water for wildlife must be sought by those with small children, or with little space or no time to carry out maintenance.

Starting small

If your only outside space is a patio, balcony or tiny roof garden it is still possible to provide clean drinking water for birds and mammals such as hedgehogs – although a balcony or roof garden may be a bit beyond the latter! A terracotta plant saucer, perhaps with a few smooth pebbles to make it attractive, will be gratefully used by your local bird population for drinking and bathing. If placed in a sunny spot, it will attract a constant stream of Blackbirds, House Sparrows, Greenfinches, Dunnocks and other common garden birds, washing their feathers, drinking at frequent intervals and providing you with endless wildlife watching. Position your pebble dish in an open area to ensure that local cats have nowhere to hide and spring an ambush. A dish of this sort outside my back door in my previous garden attracted around ten different bird species and proved a fascinating spectacle at almost any time of day. Your only commitment to such a small water feature is to ensure that it is topped up with fresh water every day, cleaned out thoroughly from time to time and de-iced in cold weather.

If birds are your priority, an alternative to a pebble dish on the ground is a purpose-built bird drinking and bathing dish or an old fashioned bird bath. Once out of fashion, these now seem to be readily available from many garden centres and bird food suppliers

Female Blackbird using a bird drinking and bathing dish

69

and they can provide a very useful source of water for birds but are of no use for aquatic wildlife. Look out for the type that can be attached to a fence, wall or post, as positioned well they have the advantage of being relatively safe from cats. They are also useful if you have limited outside space.

A water feature

The current trend for elaborate water features would seem to have little to do with wildlife gardening, but there is a case for the idea that any water in the garden is better than no water at all, as long as it is accessible to wildlife. On a visit to a large garden in North Devon, I was amazed to see a Robin repeatedly visiting a water feature in full view of many members of the public. The feature consisted of a large stone with a hole through the middle, up which water was pumped to give a pleasant trickling sound. The Robin sat in the bubbling water on top of the stone, fluffing up his feathers and enjoying a bath! If you intend to install something of this sort in your garden, try to make sure that birds at least have safe access to the water but be aware that anything with steep sides will not provide good access and could be a problem for many bird species.

A mini-pond

Whilst the alternatives described above will have some value for birds and possibly hedgehogs in your garden, they will do nothing for the insects or amphibians that rely on water. However, a mini-pond constructed in a half barrel or similar small container will often provide a home for a few frogs and Common Newts as well as some of the smaller species of damselfly, as long as they have easy access to the water.

Robin repeatedly visiting a water feature

Natural planting around a container pond

Wooden half barrels, which make very attractive 'mini-ponds', are sometimes available from garden centres but many have holes drilled in the bottom for use as planters. These are of no use for a barrel pond! If you can obtain one without holes you will find that it generally holds water very well – after all its previous use may have been as a container for rum, brandy or cider. If it has been allowed to dry out and leaks excessively it will need to be soaked in order to allow the wooden slats to absorb moisture. The easiest way to do this is to make sure it is left outside in wet, rainy weather and also to fill it up daily. The wooden slats will absorb water, expand and seal the wood as it becomes waterproof. Once this has happened, you will need to ensure that it is kept well topped up. If it is allowed to dry out it will begin to leak and you will need to go through this process again.

A mini-barrel or container pond can be placed on a patio or deck, or sunk into the ground in an out-of-the-way spot. How it is used by your garden wildlife will depend on which of these two options you chose. Do make sure it is in its final position before you fill it with water and add your plants. As these barrels have straight sides, it is necessary to make them more wildlife friendly, particularly if you are hoping for frogs or newts to use them. Those sunk into the ground are much more likely to attract these amphibians, but a barrel pond standing on a patio may attract a wide range of birds and some aquatic invertebrates, too.

Many birds will drink and bathe from a barrel pond, including Blackbirds...

...Bluetits ...

and House Sparrows.

Begin by placing a layer of garden soil in the bottom of the barrel to a depth of approximately 10 centimetres. This will provide a planting medium for your aquatic plants. Covering this with a thin layer of gravel or pea shingle will make the planting operation less messy but is not essential – the murky water will clear quite quickly. Next, around the perimeter of about one third of the barrel, place a narrow layer of pieces of turf, upside-down, to make a small platform up to where you expect your water level to be. Turf performs this function much better than soil as it holds together and creates somewhere to secure the roots of your aquatic plants.

If your pond has been sunk into the ground, this turf ledge will allow frogs and newts to get in and out safely and create a shallow area from which birds can bathe and drink. It will also provide a planting place for marginals. The pond can be filled with rain or tap water at this point and allowed to settle down for a day or two.

Planting is the next task and must be thought through carefully. The last thing you need in such a small habitat is anything invasive, but it is still important to have plants from all the categories mentioned in Chapter 4. Below are some suggestions of useful wildflowers for mini-ponds of this type. If you are intending to add non-native plants, make sure they are not invasive or too large for your small habitat.

Wild plants for mini-ponds
Emergents
Soft Rush, Lesser Spearwort
Floaters
Fringed Water Lily, Duckweed, Water Crowfoot

Water Crowfoot in a barrel pond

A barrel pond dug into a border

Marginals
Brooklime, Lesser Spearwort, Water Mint
Oxygenators
Curly Pondweed, Hornwort, Water Milfoil, Water Crowfoot

To introduce your chosen plants, simply push the roots of the oxygenators and Fringed Water Lily into the layer of soil beneath the gravel. Your chosen marginals and emergents such as Soft Rush can have their roots tucked into the turf ledge. Frogbit and Duckweed simply float decoratively on the water surface. The objective with your plants is to have a varied and attractive mix – spiky rushes contrasting with flat-leaved floaters and colourful flowering marginals.

None of these are very invasive, and a pond of this size is quite easy to maintain. Taking out excess plant growth in the autumn every year will keep your mini-pond looking good. Try to keep about two thirds of the surface water open and plant free.

If you prefer to include some non-natives, ensure that they are small and slow growing or your mini-pond will be taken over in one season. The small species of bulrush (*Typha minima*) is lovely and non-invasive, and you may like the white-flowered variety of our native Marsh Marigold. My favourite plant for a small pond like this is Water Crowfoot – an oxygenator with dense but feathery leaves creating a mass of vegetation that supports bathing birds and has lovely white flowers.

As we have already seen, a barrel pond like this will provide a small watery habitat for quite a range of aquatic wildlife as well as a place where birds will drink and bathe. However, if the pond is on a patio, rather than sunk into the ground, there will be restricted access for creatures such as frogs and newts unless you also construct a ramp of some sort at one side. This can be done, but it is generally better to assume that a patio barrel will encourage birds and damselflies, water boatmen and water beetles, rather than amphibians.

Bog gardens

Bog gardens are wetland habitats but generally do not have open water. Often they are constructed alongside a pond, using any overflow of pond water to maintain the dampness that the plants require. They have a limited

A small bog garden in a damp spot

value to the aquatic wildlife in your garden but can be useful places for growing wild marsh plants, most of which provide nectar or pollen for insects. A bog garden is, however, a useful refuge for small frogs, toads and newts emerging from your pond, providing them with sheltered hiding places when they are most vulnerable. Some species of dragon- and damselfly will lay their eggs on plants near to open water, so a bog garden can be useful in this respect too.

Bog garden construction in order to grow exotic primulas or hostas can be a complicated affair, but for the purpose of providing an additional habitat for wildlife, construction can be simplified considerably. All that is needed here is a place where water does not drain away quickly and supports plants that require a wet soil. However, the danger of a simple construction is that the soil in an area such as this can become stagnant and unhealthy. It is not enough simply to fill a hole with an old piece of pond liner and introduce marsh plants – some drainage is needed to ensure a flow of water through the area to keep the soil aerated and fragrant! This flow of water, however slow, can create a problem when a pond is constructed with a bog garden attached as water may drain from one to the other surprisingly quickly. I would always construct a boggy patch as a completely separate area, even if it is alongside a wildlife pond. Where open water and soil are connected, it is possible for water to wick out of the pond and evaporate, causing the water level in the pond to fall very rapidly as we have seen in Chapter 3.

Bog garden construction begins with digging a suitable hole, which can be alongside your pond, where it will provide a welcome additional habitat for wildlife, or it can be elsewhere in the garden if you prefer. Areas in full sun or part shade are suitable, but be aware that a bog garden in full sun is likely to dry out more quickly and will require more frequent topping up to keep the plants happy. The depth needs to be between 30 and 60 centimetres and lined with whatever you have available – an old piece of pond liner will work well, or sturdy plastic of some sort. The bog will need drainage as already mentioned, so once the liner is in place, spike it with a fork across the bottom to enable water to drain out slowly. If you wish you can now place a layer of gravel in the bottom to aid drainage further, but if your intention is to grow wildflowers such as Purple Loosestrife and Ragged Robin, this is not really necessary.

Start to backfill the hole with your garden soil, adding a little home-made compost or leaf mould if you have any as this will help to hold water. Avoid something as rich as farmyard manure as, if you intend to grow wildflowers, you may find the rich soil reduces the numbers of flowers at the expense of the foliage. At about the halfway point you may want to consider introducing a length of pipe attached to an overflow

Pond Alternatives

A bog garden with Primulas

Bog gardens can produce luxurious plant growth

from a nearby water butt. If there is no overflow facility, one can be easily made by drilling a hole near the top of the butt and fitting the end of a piece of hose pipe tightly into it. Dig the pipe into the ground, allowing the other end to come to rest inside the bog garden. Once it is in position, arrange a few stones around the open end to prevent it from becoming blocked with soil. Whenever your water butt is full, the overflow will now top up your bog garden with fresh clean rainwater. Now continue to fill the bog garden with soil until the liner is completely covered.

The bog garden can now be planted with your favourite wetland plants. See the table on page 78 for a few suggestions.

A bog garden with Primula and Ornamental Rhubarb

Adapting an existing pond

Inherited ponds can be a bonus in a new garden. However, we are much more wildlife friendly in our gardens now than in the past and many older gardens have ponds made of concrete with straight, steep sides. This makes them very unsuitable for wildlife. They may well have frogs or newts finding their way in or out, but from a bird's eye view, these ponds can be hazardous to say the least. It is very distressing to find a drowned bird in a garden pond which fell in whilst drinking and was unable to scramble out. Even worse is the sight of a dead hedgehog that has slipped in overnight. Hedgehogs are good swimmers, but if there is no obvious exit, they can tire and drown quite easily.

Straight-sided ponds can be adapted in a variety of ways. The simplest way, if the pond is not too deep, is to build up one corner with stones, soil and turf to water surface level and plant wildlife-friendly marginals. If the pond is too formal for such adaptation, and you wish to preserve the formality, a series of planting baskets with irises or other wetland plants can also provide a platform for birds to use safely, as long as these baskets are near the water's edge. They will also create a lifeline for a hedgehog that may have fallen in and an easy access point for frogs and newts.

If the pond is exceptionally deep, the only answer may be to provide a wooden ramp, weighted down on the bottom of the pond with stones or bricks. Try to arrange that the other end reaches the bank amongst thick planting.

If none of these remedies is appropriate, try providing another small pond in the garden that is safe for wildlife, and give your visitors a choice. They will certainly use the easier option for access to water.

In Conclusion

Almost everyone with a patch of garden can provide water for native wildlife. Whether it's a large wetland habitat or a mini-barrel pond, you will be creating a wonderful and important resource for all the wildlife around you that requires water for breeding, bathing or simply to drink. And don't underestimate the huge amount of pleasure that you will derive from seeing this wildlife close at hand. Hopefully you are now thinking about creating a wildlife pond somewhere in your own garden and will then soon find out for yourself just what an exciting and rewarding choice this can be, both for wildlife and us.

Hedgehogs are good swimmers, but if there is no obvious exit they can tire and drown.

Wildflowers to create a natural-looking pond

English name	Latin name	Plant Type				
		B	E	F	M	L
Amphibious Bistort	Persicaria amphibia			✿		
Arrowhead	Sagittaria sagittifolia		✿			
Bogbean	Menyanthes trifoliata			✿	✿	
Brooklime	Veronica beccabunga	✿			✿	
Bugle	Ajuga reptans	✿				
Branched Bur Reed	Sparganium erectum	✿	✿		✿	✿
Common Fleabane	Pulicaria dysenterica	✿				
Cowslip	Primula veris	✿				
Creeping Jenny	Lysimachia nummularia	✿				
Cyperus Sedge	Carex pseudocyperus	✿	✿		✿	
Duckweed	Lemna minor			✿		
Devil's Bit Scabious	Succisa pratensis	✿				
Flowering Rush	Butomus umbellatus	✿	✿		✿	
Fringed Water Lily	Nymphoides peltata			✿		
Frogbit	Hydrocharis morsus-ranae			✿		
Gipsywort	Lycopus europaeus	✿				
Greater Burnet	Sanguisorba officinalis	✿				
Greater Spearwort	Ranunculus lingua		✿		✿	✿
Hemp Agrimony	Eupatorium cannabinum	✿				
Lady's Smock	Cardamine pratensis	✿				
Lesser Bulrush	Typha angustifolia		✿		✿	✿
Lesser Spearwort	Ranunculus flammula				✿	
Marshmallow	Althaea officinalis	✿				
Marsh Marigold	Caltha palustris	✿			✿	
Marsh Woundwort	Stachys palustris	✿				
Meadowsweet	Filipendula ulmaria	✿				
Purple Loosestrife	Lythrum salicaria	✿				
Ragged Robin	Lychnis flos-cuculi	✿				
Soft Rush	Juncus effusus		✿		✿	
Hard Rush	Juncus inflexus		✿		✿	
Sweet Flag	Acorus calamus	✿	✿		✿	
Sweet Galingale	Cyperus longus		✿		✿	✿
Valerian	Valeriana officinalis	✿				
Water Avens	Geum rivale	✿				
Water Figwort	Scrophularia aquatica	✿			✿	
Water Forget-me-not	Myosotis scorpioides	✿			✿	
Water Mint	Mentha aquatica	✿			✿	
Water Plantain	Alisma plantago-aquatica	✿	✿		✿	
Water Soldier	Stratiotes aloides			✿		
Water Violet	Hottonia palustris		✿			
White Water Lily	Nyphaea alba			✿		✿
Yellow Flag	Iris pseudacorus	✿			✿	✿
Yellow Loosestrife	Lysimachia vulgaris	✿				
Yellow Water Lily	Nuphar lutea			✿		✿

B – bog garden **E** – emergent **F** – floater **M** – marginal **L** – large ponds only

Further Information

Suppliers of pond plants

Emorsgate Seeds: Limes Farm,
Tilney All Saints, Kings Lynn,
Norfolk PE34 4RT,
Tel: 01553 829028,
www.wildseed.co.uk

Habitataid: Hookgate Cottage,
South Brewham, Somerset BA10 0LQ,
Tel: 01749 812355,
www.habitataid.co.uk

British Wild Flower Plants
Main Road
North Burlingham NR13 4TA
Phone: 01603 716615
www.wildflowers.uk

Jenny Steel's website
www.wildlife-gardening.co.uk has a complete guide to wildlife gardening, including updated lists of suppliers.

Further Reading

Baines, Chris (2016) *Companion to Wildlife Gardening*. Frances Lincoln

Clegg, John (1992) *The Observer's Book of Pond Life*. Godfrey Cave

(Various authors) (2015) *Concise Pond Wildlife Guide*. Bloomsbury Natural History

Steel, Jenny (2006) *Bringing a Garden to Life*, Wiggly Wigglers

Steel, Jenny (2013) *Making Garden Meadows*, Brambleby Books

Steel, Jenny (2015) *Butterfly Gardening*, Brambleby Books

Thomas, Adrian (2010) *Gardening for Wildlife – A Complete Guide to Nature-friendly Gardening*. A & C Black, London

Other nature books by Brambleby Books

Making Garden Meadows – How to create
a natural haven for wildlife
Jenny Steel
ISBN 978 1908241 221

Butterfly Gardening – How to encourage
butterflies to your garden
Jenny Steel
ISBN 978 1908241 481

Norfolk Wildlife – A Calendar and Site Guide
Adrian M. Riley
ISBN 978 1908241 047

British and Irish Butterflies
Adrian M. Riley
ISBN 978 0955392 801

Garden Photo Shoot –
A Photographer's Yearbook of Garden Wildlife
John Thurlbourn
ISBN 978 0955392 832

Walking with Birds
Colin Whittle
ISBN 978 1908241 351

The Greater World of Little Things
Ross Gardner
ISBN 978 1908241 382

The Wild Flowers of Jersey
Deirdre Shirreffs
ISBN 978 1908241 337

Dragons and Damsels – An Identification
Guide to the British and Irish Odonata
Adrian M. Riley
ISBN 9781908241641

The Boy and the Trout
Richard ffrench-Constant
ISBN 9781908241580

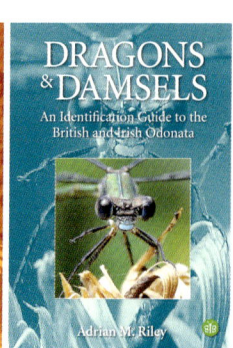

www.bramblebybooks.co.uk